Do You Know about Insects?

Buffy Silverman

Lerner Publications Company
Minneapolis

To my Bug Doctor,
Jeff, with love
-B. S.

Lerner Publications Company
A division of Lerner Publishing Group, Inc.
241 First Avenue North
Minneapolis, MN 55401 U.S.A.

Website address: www.lernerbooks.com

Library of Congress Cataloging-in-Publication Data

Silverman, Buffy.
    Do you know about insects? / by Buffy Silverman.
        p.   cm. — (Lightning bolt books™ — Meet the animal groups)
    Includes index.
    ISBN 978-0-8225-7544-3 (lib. bdg. : alk. paper)
    1. Insects—Juvenile literature. I. Title.
    QL467.2.S54 2010
    595.7—dc22   2007038931

Manufactured in the United States of America
1 2 3 4 5 6 — BP — 15 14 13 12 11 10

Contents

Insects Have Six Legs

A luna moth spreads his wings. He flies in the night. A tiny flea hops onto a dog. She sucks blood. Moths and fleas are insects. A beetle is an insect too.

How can you tell?
Insects are animals with six legs.

Count the dragonfly's legs. Is it an insect?

Insect Bodies

Insect bodies have hard outer coverings called exoskeletons. They protect their bodies. The body of an adult insect has three main parts.

The head is at the front.
The thorax is in the middle.
The abdomen is at the end.

Can you see the three main body parts on this adult wasp?

A praying mantis has huge eyes on its head. It sees a crawling caterpillar. **Watch out!**

The praying mantis eats the caterpillar.

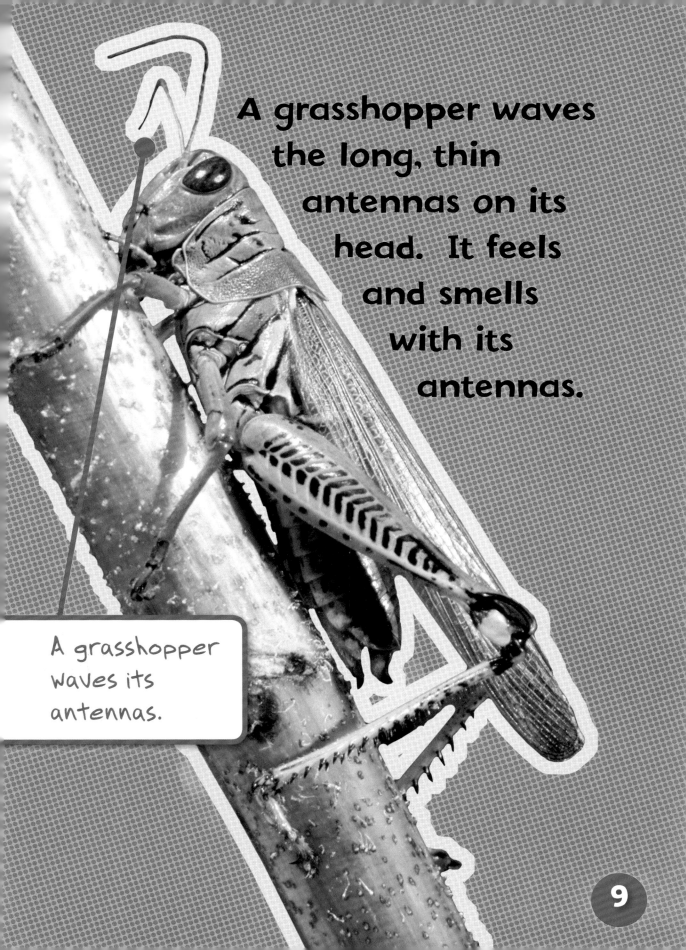

A grasshopper waves the long, thin antennas on its head. It feels and smells with its antennas.

A grasshopper waves its antennas.

An insect's wings and legs are on its thorax. Insects use their wings and legs to move.

A wasp's wings are on the middle part of its body. This part is called the thorax.

A treehopper's thorax looks like a thorn. It helps the hopper hide on a plant stem.

11

Insects breathe through openings along the thorax and abdomen.

Do you see the tiny openings on this cricket's body? Insects breathe through these openings.

The food that an insect eats is broken down in the abdomen.

Beware of the bee's stinger!

It is on the end of its abdomen. Honeybees sting to keep other animals away from their hives.

This bee is about to sting someone.

How Insects Grow

Insects begin life as eggs. A katydid lays eggs through a tube on her abdomen.

This leaf katydid is laying eggs on a log.

Ants take care of eggs in an underground nest.

A giant water bug lays eggs on her mate's back. He carries the eggs until they hatch.

Nymphs hatch from the water bug eggs. Nymphs look like their parents. But they have no wings.

This dragonfly nymph lives in a pond. It has no wings. But it can crawl underwater.

Cricket nymphs hop in a field. They eat lots of plants. The nymphs grow bigger.

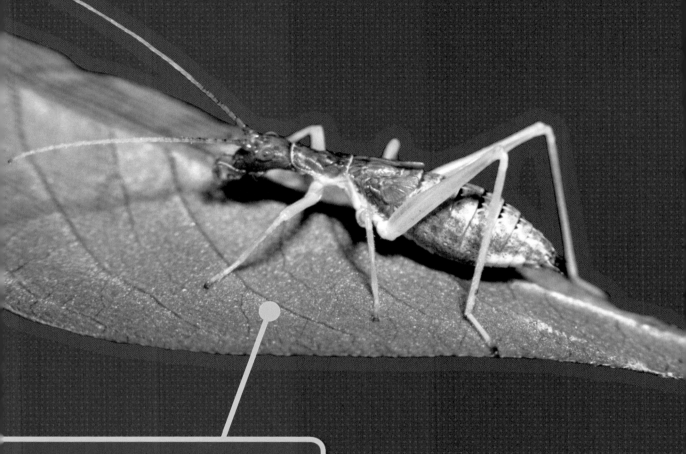

A snowy tree cricket nymph eats plants to grow.

But the nymphs' exoskeletons cannot grow. The nymphs shed their exoskeletons and grow new ones. Then they become adults.

Cricket nymphs shed their outer covering seven times or more.

Many insects grow in a different way. They look like worms when they hatch. They are called larvas.

These larvas grow in a nest made of wax. They will grow into bumblebees.

Insects lay eggs where their larvas will find food.

A ladybug lays eggs on a leaf. Soon larvas will hatch from the eggs. The larvas will hunt aphids that live on the leaves.

Larvas eat and eat. They grow fast. They shed their exoskeletons many times. Then they become pupas.

A ladybug larva eats an aphid.

Pupas grow and change inside a hard case. They come out of the case when they are adults. Then they have wings. The females can lay eggs.

Bumblebee pupas grow inside their cases.

23

Where Insects Live

Insects live almost everywhere on Earth. Millions of different insects live in rain forests. Caterpillars munch on tree leaves in the rain forest.

Caterpillars are larvas. This caterpillar will become a moth.

Honeypot ants live in the desert. These ants get extra food. When food is hard to find, they will feed their nest mates.

The abdomens of honeypot ants swell up with food.

How do these beetles live in the cold? Special chemicals inside their bodies keep them from freezing.

This red bark beetle can live through freezing winters in Alaska.

Where can you find insects?

Fireflies light up the night in this meadow.

Match the Mouths

Some insects suck liquids with their mouths. Others chew. Match the insects on page 28 with the pictures on page 29. How do their mouths help them get food?

Dragonfly nymph

Paper wasp

Butterfly

Housefly

1.

This insect shoots out its mouth. Watch it catch a fish!

This insect sips nectar from flowers.

2.

This insect's mouth is like a sponge. It soaks up spilled juice.

3.

4.

This insect chews other insects and feeds them to its young.

Check your answers on page 31

Glossary

abdomen: the end part of an insect's body

antenna: a feeler on an insect's head. An insect smells and feels with antennas.

caterpillar: the larva of a butterfly or moth

exoskeleton: the hard outer covering of an insect

insect: an animal that has six legs and three main body parts as an adult

larva: a young insect that looks like a worm and becomes a pupa

nymph: a young insect that changes gradually into an adult. A nymph looks like a small adult, but it does not have wings.

pupa: a young insect in the stage of life between larva and adult. A pupa does not eat.

shed: throw off

thorax: the middle part of an insect's body. Legs and wings are attached to the thorax.

Further Reading

BOOKS

Piehl, Janet. *Flying Mosquitoes*. Minneapolis: Lerner Publications Company, 2007.

Rockwell, Anne. *Bugs Are Insects*. New York: HarperCollins, 2001.

Waxman, Laura Hamilton. *Monarch Butterflies*. Minneapolis: Lerner Publications Company, 2003.

WEBSITES

Alien Empire
http://www.pbs.org/wnet/nature/alienempire/
Enter the world of insects, and see how they live and survive.

Going Bug-gy!
http:teacher.scholastic.com/activities/bugs
Play games and learn more about amazing insects.

Answer key for pages 28–29:
A paper wasp is shown in number 4.
A dragonfly nymph is shown in number 1.
A butterfly is shown in number 3.
A housefly is shown in number 2.

Index

Photo Acknowledgments

The images in this book are used with the permission of: © Royalty-Free/CORBIS, pp. 1, 2; © age fotostock/ SuperStock, pp. 5, 7, 17, 22; © Francesco Tomasinelli/Photo Researchers, Inc., p. 8; © Jeff Daly/Visuals Unlimited, Inc., p. 9; © Paulo De Oliveira/Taxi/Getty Images, p. 10; © Valorie Hodgson/Visuals Unlimited, Inc., p. 11; © Jerome Wexler/Visuals Unlimited, Inc., p. 12; © Hans Pfletschinger/Peter Arnold, Inc., pp. 13, 19; © Michael & Patricia Fogden/CORBIS, p. 14; © George Grall/National Geographic/Getty Images, p. 15; © Dwight Kuhn, pp. 16, 20, 23; © Bill Beatty/Visuals Unlimited, Inc., pp. 18, 26; © Dorling Kindersley/Getty Images, p. 21; © Margarette Mead/The Image Bank/Getty Images, p. 24; © Mitsuhiko Imamori/Minden Pictures, p. 25; © Color-Pic, Inc./Animals Animals, p. 27; © Bruce Coleman Inc./Alamy, pp. 28 (top left), 29 (top left); © Gerry Ellis/Minden Pictures, pp. 28 (bottom left), 29 (bottom left); © Stephen Dalton/ NHPA/Photoshot, pp. 28 (bottom right), 29 (top right); © iStockphoto.com/Phil Jackson, pp. 28 (top right), 29 (bottom right); © iStockphoto.com/step2626, p. 30; © iStockphoto.com/Dragan Krstic, p. 31.

Front Cover: © Gail Shumway/Photographer's Choice/Getty Images (ants); © iStockphoto.com/Willi Schmitz (ladybug); © iStockphoto.com/Pavel Lebedinsky (beetle); © iStockphoto.com/Tomasz Pietryszek (wasp); © iStockphoto.com/Chen Chih-Wen (praying mantis); © iStockphoto.com/Dirk Rietschel (house-fly); © iStockphoto.com/Natasha Litova (bumblebee).